EXPRESSING MY FEELINGS IN HAWAII

Written and Illustrated by Bettyfern Bluth McNally

Thank you
to

Pat McNally, Miceala Shocklee and
Martha Troedson for their assistance
with my book.

I wish to dedicate to all the children in the
world as they learn to express their feelings.

How excited the six children were to plan for an island adventure. They wanted to fly to an island to explore, see and discover the islands activities, especially the sports. First, they were undecided, but then they decided to visit just two islands, Oahu and the Big Island. The children who could read started to read to the children who couldn't read. All six were interested to learn and see what the Hawaiian Islands are. They learned the Hawaiian Islands are made up of a group of islands in the Pacific Ocean. All of the islands have been formed in the past by volcanoes. The islands have a pleasant, warm, sunny climate.

Feelings: excited, undecided, decided, interested
Senses: see
Place: home

OAHU
HAWAII

Sunday

Their plane left the airport for the Hawaiian Islands. They were all anxious and a bit impatient to arrive. So that they would not be bored on the plane, each child had packed a backpack with fun items for touching and playing. When they were packing Kyle said, " I wish to take my travel chess to play with Lily." He was so thoughtful to bring it in his backpack for the two of them. Lily said, "I wish to bring some favorite books to read." Kate said, "I wish to bring colors and paper to draw." Ella and Lacy said, "We wish to take our dolls." They had packed extra milk and soft toys for Baby L. Ann.

Feelings: anxious, impatient, bored, thoughtful
Senses: touching
Place: plane

L
K
K
L
E
LA

When they all arrived at the airport on the island of Oahu, a smiling, happy, friendly lady wearing a muumuu greeted them. This is a long, loose fitting dress made of brightly colored material. She put a necklace of flowers around their necks. She said, "Aloha." This means hello, goodbye or love. Ella, Lacy and baby L. Ann were feeling bashful when she put the flowered leis around their necks. The flowers smelled like perfume. All the children were very excited!

Feelings: happy, friendly, love, bashful, excited
Senses: smelled
Place: Oahu airport

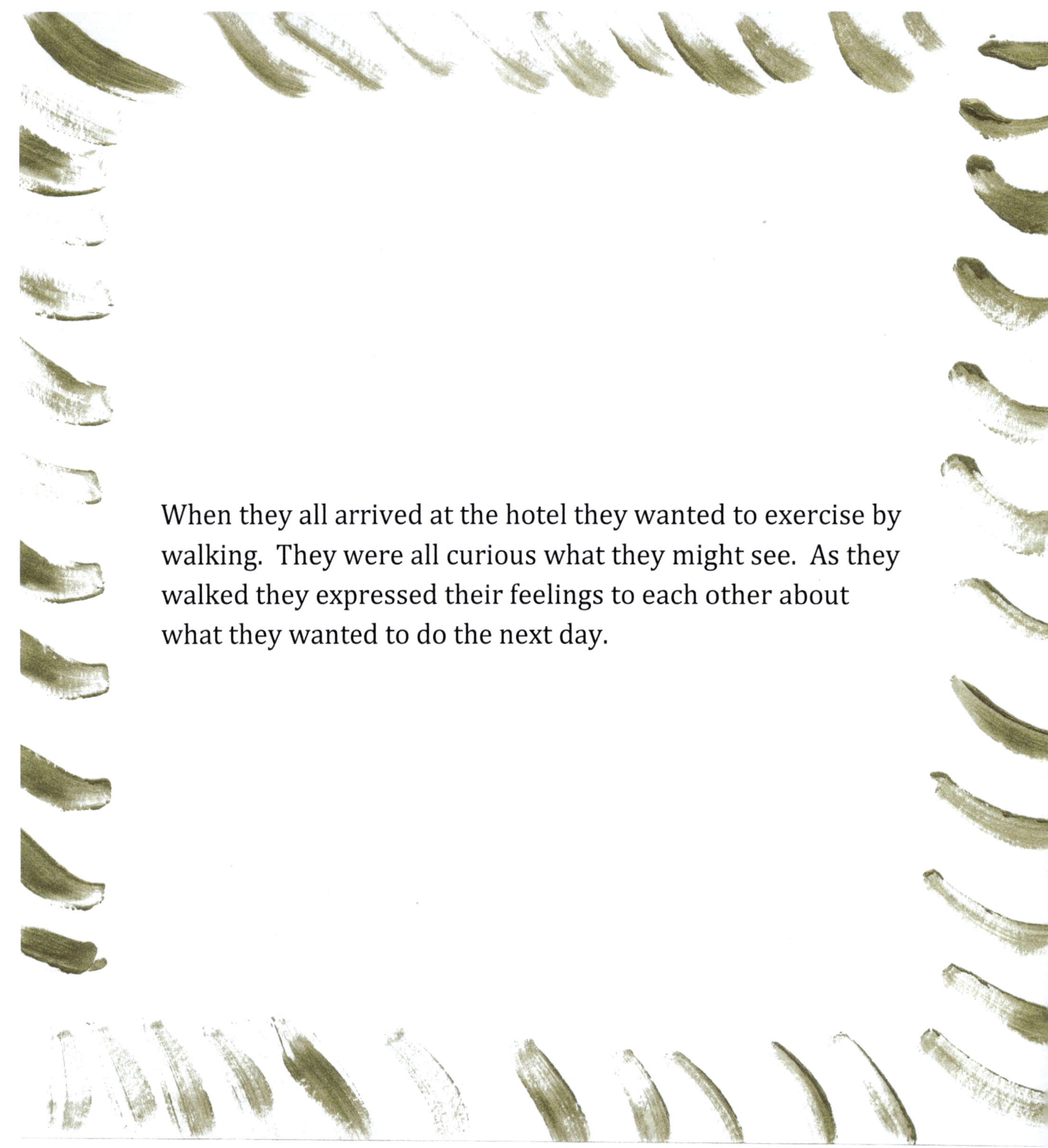

When they all arrived at the hotel they wanted to exercise by walking. They were all curious what they might see. As they walked they expressed their feelings to each other about what they wanted to do the next day.

Ella said, "I want to take my sand toys and go see the beach."
Lacy said, "Me too, let's get a big umbrella to shade us."
Baby L. Ann said, "Coo."
Kyle and Kate said, "We want to rent a surfboard and explore the ocean waters."
Kyle said, "I want to go together so I don't feel lonely when I am out in the water."
I want to share the surfboard with Kate."
Lily said, "I want to take sailing lessons."

Feelings: curious, lonely
Senses: see
Place: hotel

They started on their walk. They were very excited to see a shop that had snorkeling equipment for rent. Kyle and Kate were eavesdropping on what the customers were asking and ordering for their snorkeling and surfboard adventures.

Their day was almost over so they each ordered special Oahu ice cream.

Kyle said, "I wish to order mint chip."

Kate said, "I wish to order chocolate."

Lacy said, "I wish to order strawberry."

Lily said, "I wish to order coffee ice cream."

Ella said, "I wish to order vanilla with lots of sprinkles."

Baby L. Ann said, "Coo."

It tasted delicious!!!

They carried their ice cream cones to the sandy beach to watch the sunset.

Feelings: excited

Senses: see, tasted, hear (eavesdropping)

Place: ice cream store

Everyone was fascinated at the beauty of the sunset in Oahu.
After the sun went down it got dark. Baby L. Ann, Lacy and
Ella became frightened. The older three children felt
confident that they could find their way back to the hotel.
Once they were back it was time for dinner.
They tasted some of the local food of the island. Exploring
and discovering special food of the island was fun for them.
They shared plates of mangoes, figs, pineapples, passion
fruit, guavas, coconut, plums and kumquats. For dessert they
ate Macadamia Nut Cookies.

Feelings: frightened, confident
Senses: tasted
Place: hotel

MONDAY

They woke up excited to start their day. For breakfast, they all had some toasted Hawaiian Bread with fresh locally grown fruit. They expressed to each other what they wanted to do that day. Feeling energetic, they all decided to ride bikes by the popular Waikiki Beach. They wanted to explore the area by their hotel. On their bike ride they could see the beautiful ocean and hear the crashing waves.

Feelings: excited, energetic, decided
Senses: see, hear
Place: Waikiki Beach

Riding along the beach and smelling the beach air was fun. Lily was frustrated when her bike chain fell off. She was mad at first, then she felt sad. She was sad and disappointed. She felt guilty because she thought she was spoiling the bike ride for the other children.

All the children tried to fix it, but they all became exasperated and disappointed. Lily was apologetic to all the other children. Frustrated, they decided to return the bikes to the bike shop.

Feelings: frustrated, mad, sad, disappointed, guilty, exasperated, disappointed, apologetic, decided
Senses: smelling
Place: Waikiki Beach

Ella said, "I am ready to go to the ocean and play with my sand toys under an umbrella."
Lacy said, "Me too."
Baby L. Ann said, "Coo."
On the sunny beach, all the children put on sunscreen and long sleeved t-shirts to protect their skin from the sun touching their skin. Kyle and Kate were happy that they rented the last surfboard at the shop. In the water, Kyle was feeling aggressive to ride on his surfboard. He felt proud when he rode the waves. Kate was determined to be on top of the board.

Feelings: happy, aggressive, proud
Senses: touching
Place: the beach

Unfortunately, Lily was jealous of Kate's new bathing suit. She felt relaxed after reading her book on the quiet beach. When she felt hot she splashed in the ocean with Ella, Lacy and Baby L. Ann. The ocean tasted salty just like the ocean at home.

All six children liked the ocean smelling so fresh and looking so clean. Kate cut her leg on the surfboard. All the other five children were very sympathetic.

Feelings: jealous, relaxed, sympathetic
Senses: tasted, smelling
Places: on the sand and in the ocean

Lily said, "I want to take a hula lesson." This is a Polynesian dance using hip and hand movements. Lily said, "I want to explore and discover the island dances."
Lily had brought her grass skirt to wear because she had taken hula lessons back home. They were all curious and wanted to see this Hawaiian dance. They decided to go with Lily and watch her hula. Lily felt self-conscious, but she was confident and determined she could do it.
The teacher wore a muumuu and the men played their ukuleles.

Feelings: curious, decided, self-conscious, confident, determined
Senses: see, hear (ukuleles)
Place: hula lesson

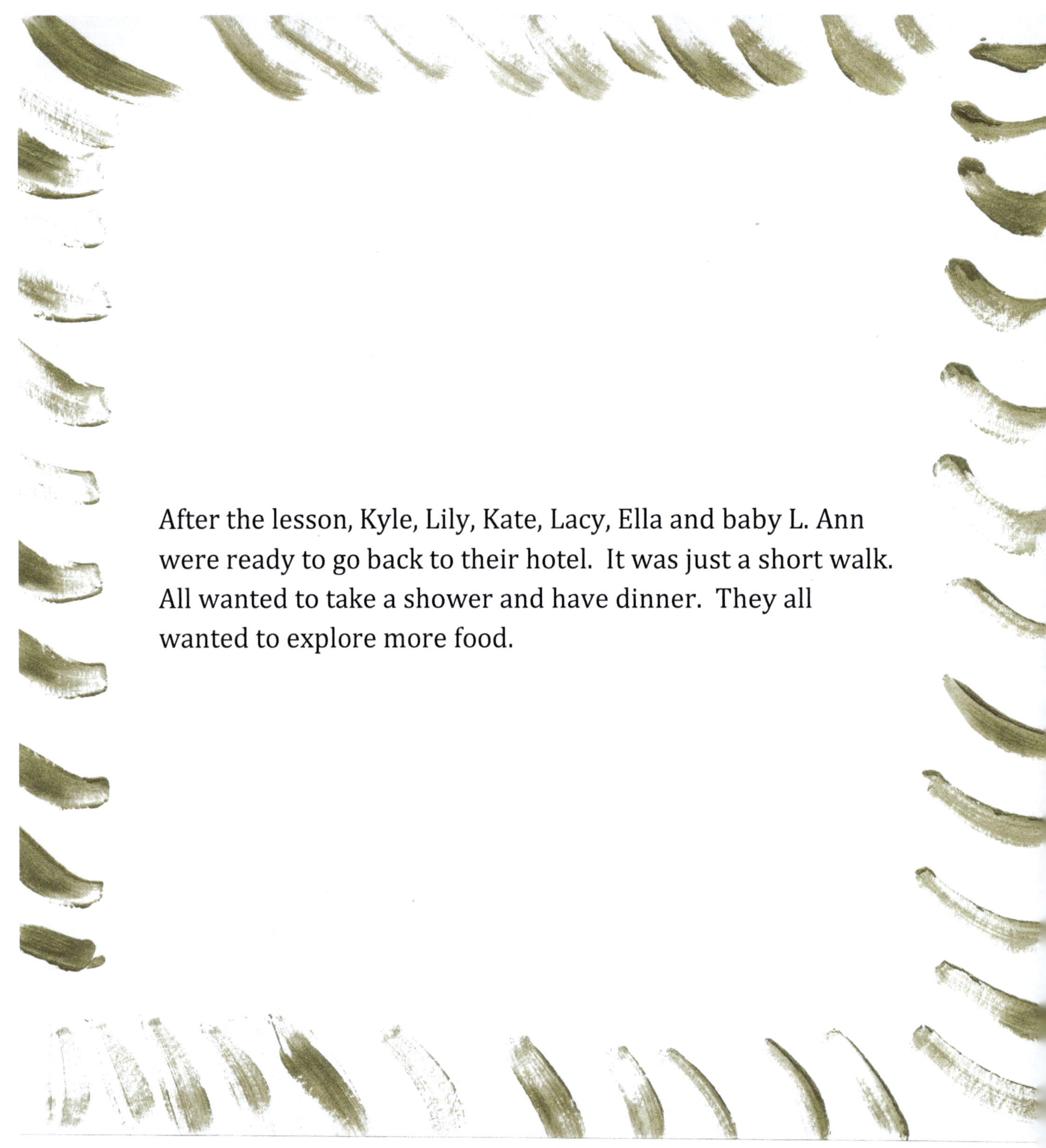

After the lesson, Kyle, Lily, Kate, Lacy, Ella and baby L. Ann
were ready to go back to their hotel. It was just a short walk.
All wanted to take a shower and have dinner. They all
wanted to explore more food.

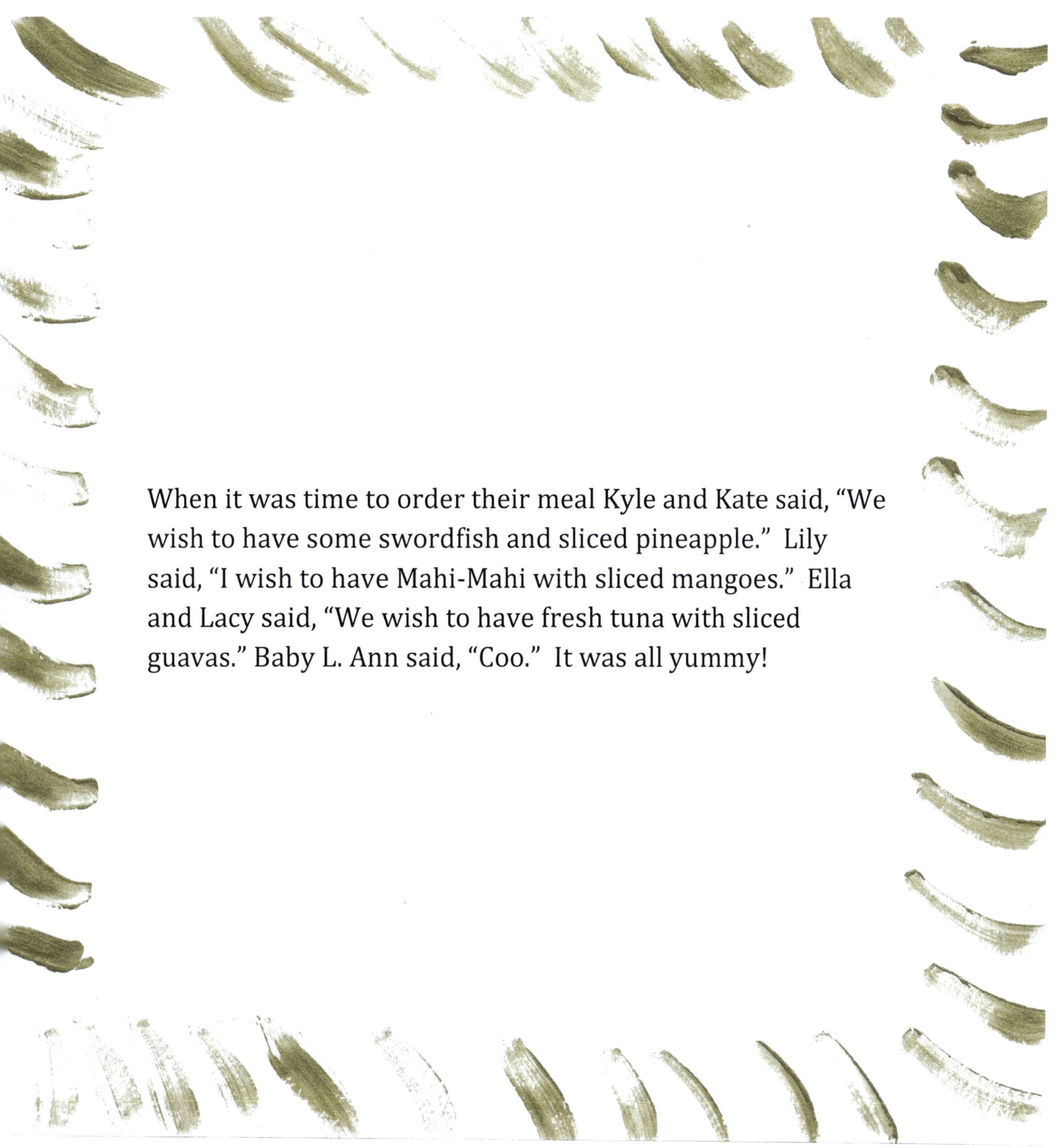

When it was time to order their meal Kyle and Kate said, "We wish to have some swordfish and sliced pineapple." Lily said, "I wish to have Mahi-Mahi with sliced mangoes." Ella and Lacy said, "We wish to have fresh tuna with sliced guavas." Baby L. Ann said, "Coo." It was all yummy!

TUESDAY

Everyone was up early ready to start the day. For breakfast, they all had fresh local fruit and mango bread. This is bread made with mashed mangos. Each child wanted to express what they wanted to explore that day.

Kyle said, "I wish to hike by the volcano mountain Diamond Head."

Lily said, "I wish to take sailing lessons."

Kate said, "I wish to explore Pearl Harbor."

Lacy and Ella said, "I wish to explore the Polynesian Cultural Center."

Baby L. Ann said, "Coo."

Off they went to hike to do Kyle's idea of exploring around Diamond Head. It is 762 feet tall. They went to the Diamond Head State Monument public park to catch the trail.

Everyone was excited when they could see the long coastline of Oahu. Beautiful!

Feeling: excited
Senses: see, taste
Place: Diamond Head

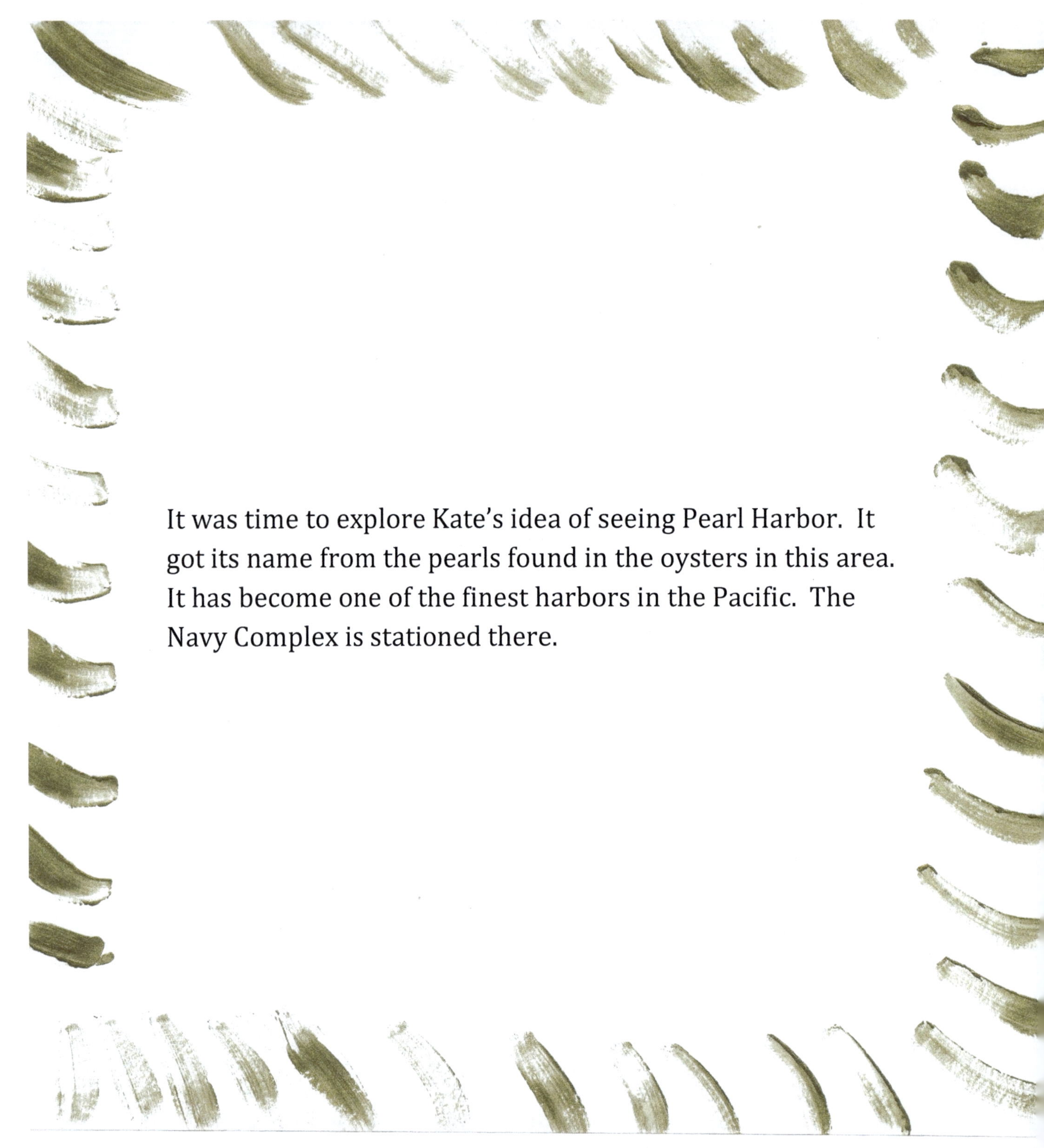

It was time to explore Kate's idea of seeing Pearl Harbor. It got its name from the pearls found in the oysters in this area. It has become one of the finest harbors in the Pacific. The Navy Complex is stationed there.

It was exciting to visit museums, memorials and memories
that are there with information about WWII. For many
people they felt sad on this visit.

Feelings: exciting, sad
Senses: seeing
Place: Pearl Harbor

Four of the children felt happy to go on an outrigger. Lily
decided instead to take a sailing lesson. Kyle wanted to go
fishing. They planned to meet at the Waikiki Aquarium after
their various activities.

Feeling: decided
Senses: happy
Places: on an outrigger, sailboat and fishing in the ocean

At the aquarium they were happy to see crabs, jellyfish, small sharks, turtles, monk seals and beautiful colors of the Hawaiian reef fish. No one was allowed to touch the reefs because the reefs would stop growing.

Feeling: happy
Senses: see, touch
Place: aquarium

It was late and everyone wanted dinner. It was time to explore more of the island food.

Kyle said, "I went fishing today." He shocked everyone with the fish he caught. The hotel chef prepared Kyle's fresh fish for dinner. It smelled delicious! All were so surprised! At dinner they each expressed what to do the next day. They voted to go in the morning to Lacy and Ella's suggestion of exploring the Polynesian Cultural center. After that they would fly to the Big Island.

Feelings: shocked, surprised
Senses: smelled
Place: dinner

WEDNESDAY

Each child packed and hurried to the Polynesian Cultural Center to see the separate villages dedicated to seven island groups. There they could see traditional crafts and activities. There was dancing and delicious food in each village. The children were shocked to see fire walking.

Feeling: shocked
Senses: see
Place: Polynesian Cultural Center

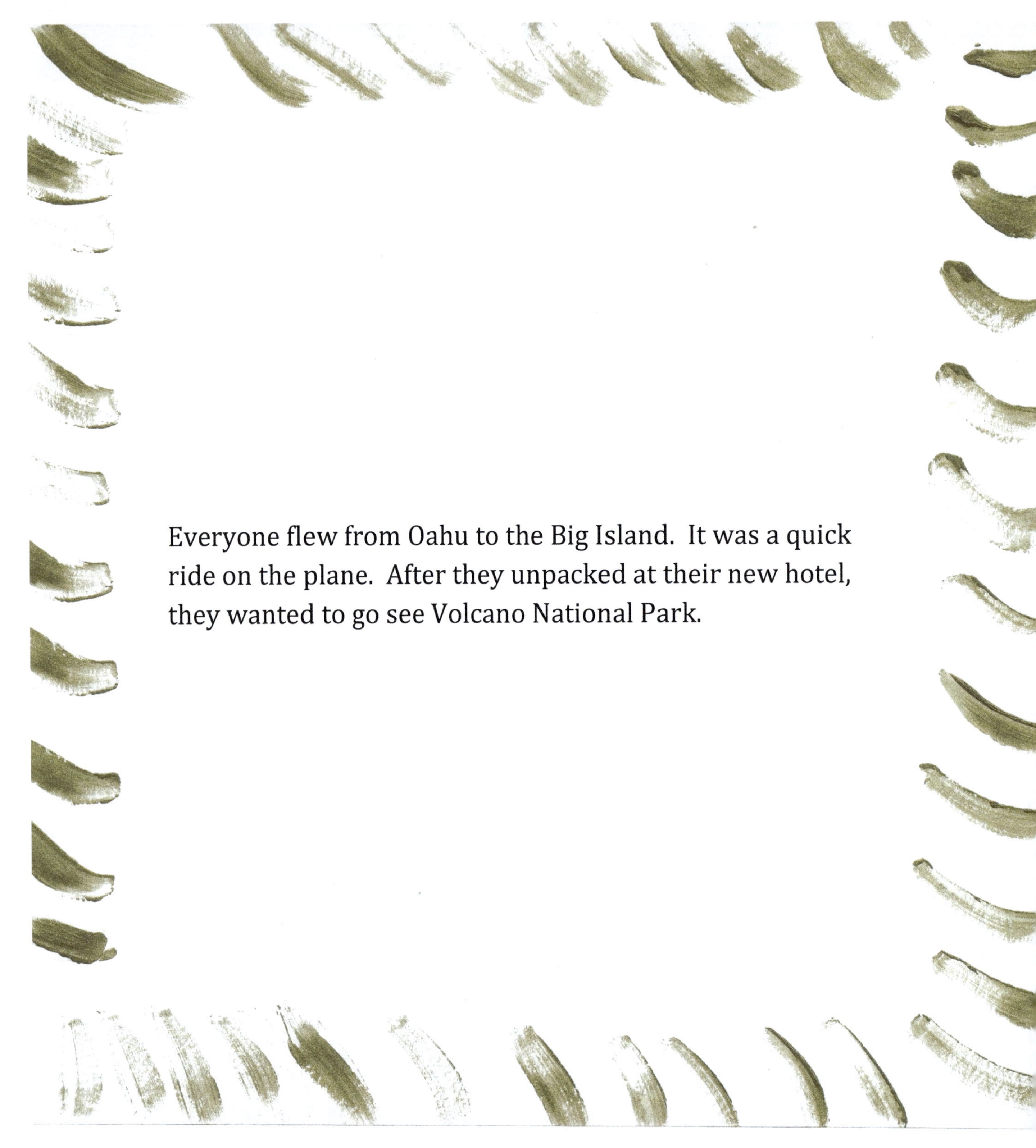

Everyone flew from Oahu to the Big Island. It was a quick ride on the plane. After they unpacked at their new hotel, they wanted to go see Volcano National Park.

They read that there were steaming craters there. They could all see the glow of the lava. They were curious as they had never seen anything like this before.

Feeling: curious
Senses: see
Place: Volcano National Park

Each of the children wanted to go to the beach for an afternoon of snorkeling. They put on their goggles and flippers so they could see all the different colors of the local fish. The warm ocean made them feel calm. What a great first day on the Big Island!
That evening for dinner, each ate local fish with sliced fruit. It was early to bed so they could be fresh for more adventures tomorrow.

Feeling: calm
Senses: see
Place: Big Island

THURSDAY

The children were up early to go see a large black sand beach. This is an area of little sand pieces from once molten lava that gives it this color. The water was very rough so they all decided to return and play all afternoon at the beach by their hotel.

Feeling: decided
Senses: see
Place: black sand beach

After they had tasted a delicious dinner of local fish, sliced fruit and Macadamia Nut Ice Cream, they discussed what to explore tomorrow.

Friday would be their last day on the island. It was decided to go to an early dinner at the local luau.

Feeling: decided
Senses: tasted
Place: hotel for dinner

FRIDAY

Each child was not sure what a luau was, except that it is a fun Hawaiian feast. There they saw dancing, special luau food and hula costumes. They heard ukulele music and chants. Each child decided to order a juice first. The juice choices were pineapple, papaya, mango and coconut. They ate cooked pig that was cooked in an underground oven. There was also salmon, rice noodles and poi. Poi is a thick paste that is eaten with your fingers. For dessert they all had to taste coconut flavored custard pudding.

Feeling: decided
Senses: taste, hear (ukulele music)
Place: luau

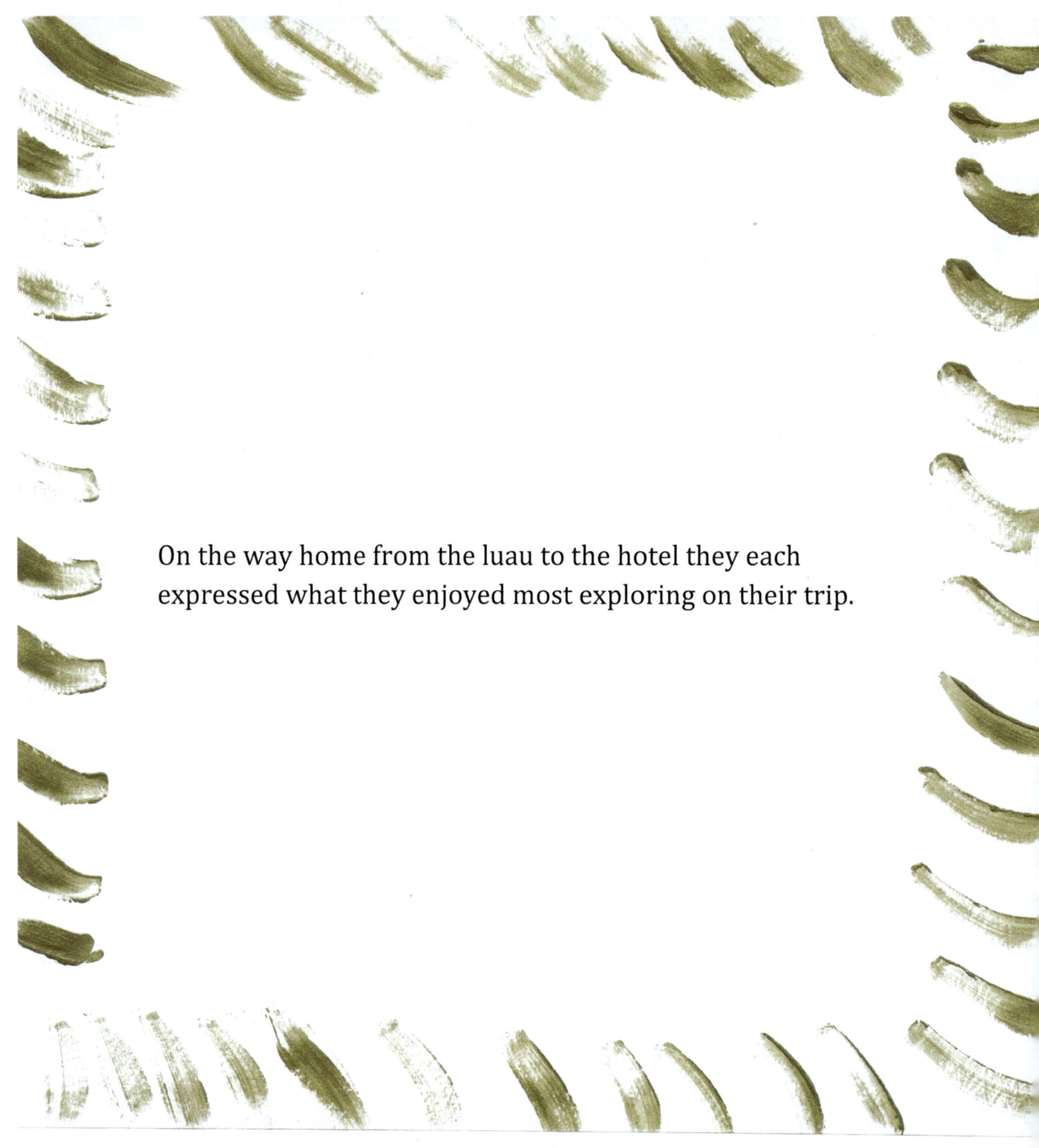

On the way home from the luau to the hotel they each expressed what they enjoyed most exploring on their trip.

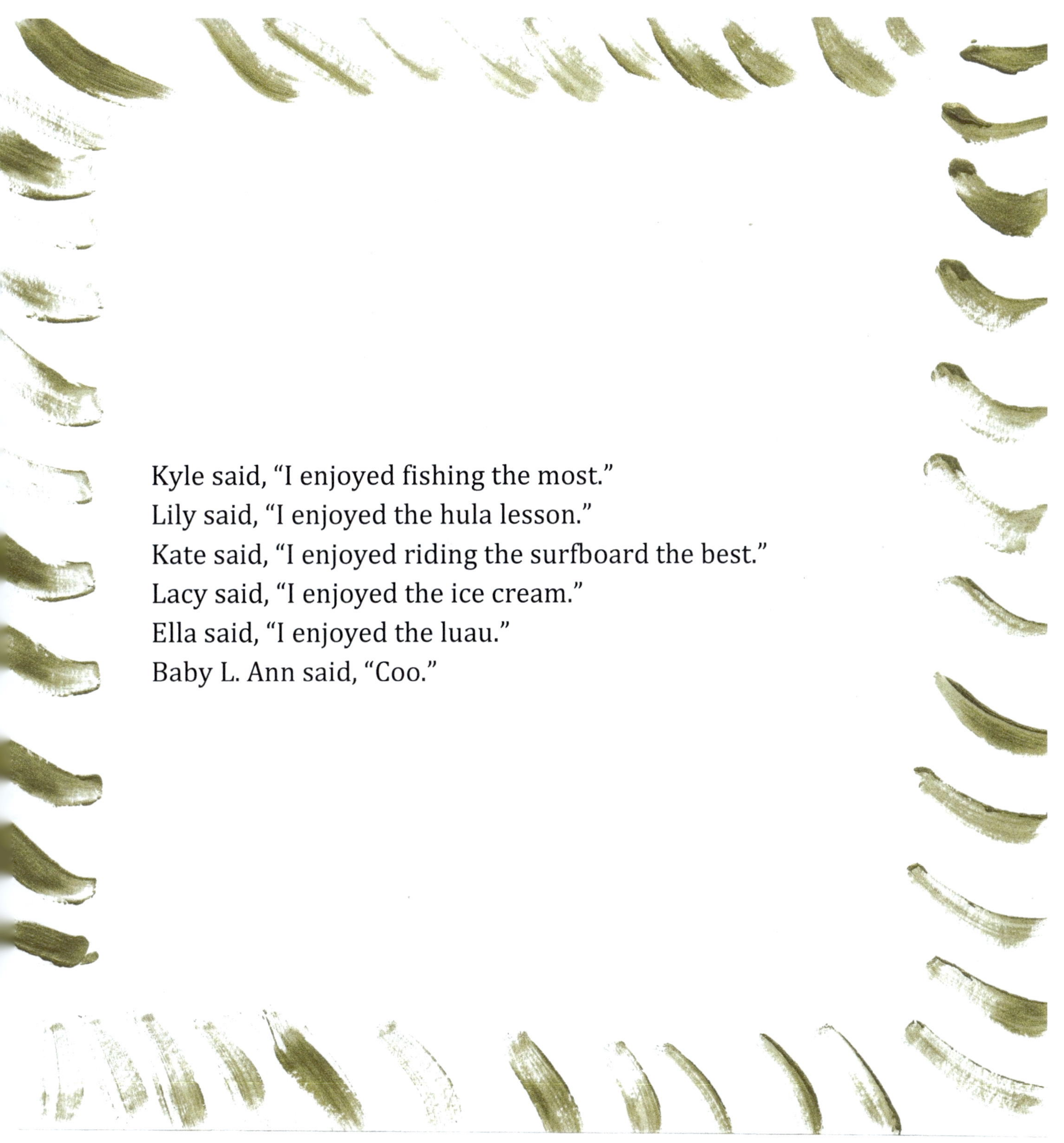

Kyle said, "I enjoyed fishing the most."

Lily said, "I enjoyed the hula lesson."

Kate said, "I enjoyed riding the surfboard the best."

Lacy said, "I enjoyed the ice cream."

Ella said, "I enjoyed the luau."

Baby L. Ann said, "Coo."

 At night, they could hear the crashing waves outside their windows. The children wondered if they would remember this crashing wave sound at home. Safe at home, they were all so happy to be in their own beds. Yes, they could hear the crashing wave sounds in their ears from the Hawaiian Islands. It was a beautiful trip for exploring and expressing.

Feeling: happy
Senses: hear
Place: in their own bed

What an adventure!!!